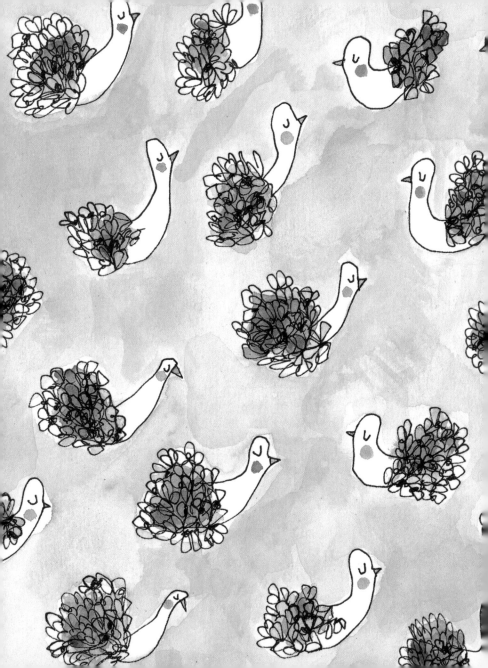

RELAX

A Little Book of Calm

Meredith Gaston

Hardie Grant

BOOKS

DEAREST YOU,

Welcome to this little book of calm. I invite you into these pages and feel so glad you have joined me here. Breathe gently in and out, take your time, and enjoy a little moment for yourself now.

The art of relaxation is a joy to explore and will imbue your life with more peace, energy and fulfilment than ever before. Our modern world is preoccupied with movement and productivity. What if a new model of existence were built around celebrating stillness, rest and relaxation in equal measure: a model supportive of our collective wellbeing, comfort and joy? ... May we embrace new, life-changing possibilities now and be the change we wish to see in our world.

Join me as we discover how slowing down and learning to soothe, settle and reaffirm ourselves enables us to move so much more smoothly and comfortably through our lives. Invite ease and grace into your days. Explore the power of sustainable personal energy and vitality built on a beautiful balance of giving and receiving, work, rest and play. Look more closely and lovingly at the ways you live your life, and learn to draw with confidence on your own deep wellspring of inner wisdom.

As you move through this book, you will find prose, prayers and affirmations on the subject of relaxation to nurture and inspire you. Allow your heart and mind to open to new ways of being as you create a calm and nourishing life – a relaxing way of living you might never have thought possible.

May this little book gift you with greater faith in yourself and the beauty of life.

Love always,
Meredith x

CONTENTS

ENJOYING THIS BOOK

This little book is composed of ten inspirational chapters
on cultivating relaxation, a practice that can help us
feel more peaceful, balanced and energised with each
new day. Embracing a calm life involves caring for
ourselves and each other with gentleness. It involves
slowing and quietening down to enjoy each moment to
the fullest, and harnessing the infinite wisdom within
and around us. Choosing to relax encompasses thinking
calmly, treading gently and speaking softly. It involves
seeing with compassion and clarity, and simplifying our
lives for greater pleasure and peace.

Choosing relaxation means nurturing our personalised foundation of wellbeing, a foundation that supports and sustains us as we go about our daily lives. Our wellbeing encompasses the thoughts we choose to think, the words we speak and the actions we take in each moment. Indeed, the art of wellbeing is so fundamental and all encompassing that it is not just a part of life but a way of life.

Taking care of our wellbeing through relaxation elevates all parts of our life experience. As we cultivate a sense of calm within and around us, we are gifted with greater health, resilience and inner peace. Our relationships and communications with others soften and strengthen, and we finesse our approach to balancing work, rest and play.

Life can become very busy. Unless we have our wits about us, we can be swept away at a pace that is very unnatural to us as profoundly creative and sensitive human beings. Yet, we always have the power to see and choose differently. Choosing to relax in daily life offers us the breathing space and tranquillity we seek. When we are rested and relaxed, we may come to life with true energy and vibrancy, creating lives that become pleasures for ourselves to live and gifts in which others can share. Bringing peace to the way we communicate and move about life, we soothe ourselves and all others with whom we share our world. Living peacefully, we live by joyous, gentle example.

Please enjoy these words and pictures, affirmations and little prayers. You may like to read this book from cover to cover or dip in and out of its pages at your whim. Please note that the word 'prayer' has been thoughtfully reclaimed from any conventional or specific context. I see prayers as emanations from our hearts: little conversations with the energy of life from which we spring and to which we return. The prayers in this book are expressions of commitment to ourselves: celebrations that show gratitude for life and living. I encourage you to draw inspiration from these prayers, embellishing them and making them your own.

Living calmly is possible for all of us. Within each one of us exists a natural balance. This is not something we need to 'find'; it is an innate essence quite simply awaiting our acknowledgement and enjoyment. As human beings we require peace and rest, and quietness and reflection, in equal measure with dynamic action. Choosing relaxation allows us to nurture the Yin to our Yang, supporting the expression of our unique energy, and nourishing our inner world: our true home.

Please remember that relaxation is a practice that with gentleness, quiet perseverance and patience becomes a natural state of being. Oftentimes we are the ones standing in our own way with outworn, self-limiting thoughts and beliefs about the way our lives 'should' be. When we change the way we look at life, life changes. Liberating ourselves so we can relax is a wonderful gift.

I encourage you never to underestimate the power of self-care and mindful living, and to have deep faith in your natural capacity for experiencing peace and calm in daily life. As we choose to relax, we imbue each day with tranquillity, allowing life to become a joy. Each one of us can cultivate calm to experience a more uplifting and harmonious life: a life in which we free ourselves to be just as we are, create positive change, care for ourselves unconditionally, and flourish gently in peace. The power of choosing relaxation extends beyond our personal realities, as it involves being part of a collective, positive movement towards heaven on earth. May we see that the intimate experience of peace for which we yearn begins right here, with and within us.

EXPLORING
THE ART OF
RELAXATION

There is an art to peaceful living. Most of us weren't taught an appreciation for relaxation, let alone the skills to cultivate and embody it in daily life. The joyous art of relaxation involves surrender, faith, perspective and tenderness. It involves knowing and honouring our sacred selves, and learning to nurture a state of ease for our spirits through caring for our minds and bodies each day.

There will always be another to-do list once our current list is ticked off. If we don't choose to relax now – relax as life happens, making time each day to savour peace, flow and rest – we quite simply never will. The time to relax is now. In this present moment. And in each and every present moment we have. If continually choosing relaxation seems unrealistic or even impossible for you right now, the exciting news is that with practice, time and care, each one of us can cultivate the art of relaxation and profoundly transform our experience of life as we know it.

Relaxation is not passive; it is a conscious form of self-care that enhances every aspect of our wellbeing. Relaxation is active: we must become aware of, and present to, the moments of peace we consciously stitch into the patchwork of our days, easing and elevating our experience of life.

Teacher David Hawkins powerfully refers to 'a continual willingness to let things go as they arise'. This allows us to clear our mental, physical, spiritual and emotional caches through constant, conscious attention. If we wish to know relaxation, we are wise to accept, forgive and release things as they happen rather than tire ourselves with rumination and overthinking.

Why create unnecessary stress for ourselves in life by holding on when we can let go? Let go of our self-limiting beliefs. Let go of our grudges and unwillingness to forgive ourselves and others. Let go of our perfectionism, our need to be right and our need for others' approval. Let go of our guilt, resentment, bitterness and fear. By letting go of these exhausting frequencies that block our energy and disconnect us from the flow of life, we can experience the freedom of true inner peace. The heartfelt bliss of relaxation.

With practice, as our minds and bodies let go and find states of ease, we may come to experience relaxation as a fortifying sense of joy. This intimate, personal joy becomes a blessing we may freely share with others.

I see the frequency of joy as an expression of the divine order and harmony resounding in all life. Every leaf, snowflake, wave, human body and fragment of creation is part of a greater intelligence: a holy symmetry and natural law. If we are moving upstream with no ease and grace, and disconnected from the flow of life, we naturally begin to feel that life is against us.

This belief perpetuates our discomfort and the very negative feelings and experiences upon which we are choosing to focus and about which we choose to complain. Unless we cultivate relaxation, we become hardened to life, and life becomes hard for us.

To relax is to actively invite greater peace, nourishment and contentment into our lives. Choosing to relax, and learning to relax even in the face of the intensity, absurdity and adversity of life, is a commitment to ourselves, each other and our earth. The energy we create and emanate matters, as we are all twinkling stars in one and the same great constellation. We are more connected and reliant upon each other than we might care to understand.

With the thoughts we choose to think and the ways we choose to live our lives, we contribute not only to our own health and happiness but to that of those with whom we share our lives. Personally accepting this truth, we become responsible for ourselves and our energetic footprint. As we relax, we contribute to releasing collective tension and stress. We live and breathe as examples of lightness and peace. With our own relaxation, we create positive change within and around us in profound and inspiring ways, actively contributing to the creation of heaven on earth.

AFFIRMATIONS

Caring for myself with love inspires
me to feel calm.

As I relax, I invite more peace
and joy into my life.

I willingly let go and embrace my life.

JOURNAL PROMPTS

My definition of relaxation is ...

I feel most relaxed when ...

I can always intercept stressful
thoughts with relaxing ones such as ...

PRAYER

I feel thankful for every relaxing
moment that I have.

Help me to see gently, tread
lightly and act lovingly as I walk
my path in peace.

FINDING EASE
AND GRACE

Inviting a sense of ease and grace into our lives
through relaxation elevates our wellbeing. When
we relax, dots connect in all parts of our lives very
naturally, smoothing, simplifying and crystallising
our relationships with ourselves, each other
and life. Opportunities arrive in perfect time,
supportive people enter our worlds and friendships
blossom. Projects proceed with far less fuss and
our inspiration flows freely and effortlessly. As we
embrace relaxation, our productivity and abundance
increase, our health flourishes and our happiness
is heartfelt. As we learn to relax, we quite simply
choose to release resistance and become one with
the rhythm of life.

Sufi mystic Rumi directs our attention to a timeless and eternal river that dances within us, a river that moves our soul. When we choose to live in harmony with ourselves and nature, we flow with the river of life. We experience daily life anew, powered by love in a spirit of gratitude and humility. As we relax and dance with life, heavenly serendipity becomes ours to enjoy, not by chance but by choice.

To flow with life requires that we agree to relinquish the illusion of control to which we all cling, albeit unwittingly and always in vain. The false belief that we control life creates great fear, stress, disappointment and disillusionment for us. With a little effort, however, we can quite simply shift our perspective. Rather than seeking to control life, we can control our thoughts about it.

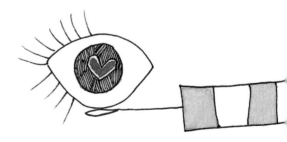

Choosing to think positive, uplifting and supportive thoughts connects us with the tremendous and limitless energy of life. Think just one positive thought and allow the universe to return it to you multiplied.

Be humbled by the perfection of nature's way and the continual unfolding of miracles around you. Adopt a sense of active participation in and proactive co-creation of your life while leaving respectful spaciousness for mystery and wonder, spontaneity and divine magic. We can be curious, open-minded and open-hearted, allowing life to move through us and inspire us at every turn. We needn't feel pressured to know all the answers, but truly knowing ourselves as we travel is our greatest treasure. As we slow down and take true care of ourselves, living each moment with mindful and loving attention, life quite simply becomes a joy. The infinite gifts already and always in our midst can capture our loving attention at last, filling us with a sense of richness.

Celebrated Taoist philosopher Lao Tzu famously wrote that 'Life is a series of natural and spontaneous changes. Don't resist them; that only creates sorrow. Let reality be reality. Let things flow naturally forward in whatever way they like.' His beautiful words offer profound and timeless wisdom for us as we navigate life to the very best of our ability in our uncertain world. A world we can still choose to see and experience as brimming with promise, mystery and beauty. A world in which we are being called to tend lovingly to our personal, communal and earthly gardens.

While letting things flow forward in any way they please might sound terrifying, choosing not to attach our hearts and minds to expectations and outcomes is something we can all do. Simply doing our best, loving life and letting life love us back relieves the tension of over-complication, freeing us to experience life in delightful new ways.

Godmother of self-care Louise Hay suggested that the word 'stress' is bandied about so much in modern life that it has become a bit of a cop out.

We go about saying, 'I'm so stressed',
'This is so stressful', scattering our
experience of stress while forging ahead,
often doing very little to truly understand
and decrease our personal tension.

We know that stress is the dominant cause of disease in our bodies and unrest in our minds. The statistics around stress are staggering and require our wholehearted attention. We must reaffirm our position daily and assert our unwillingness to be victimised by an exquisitely unpredictable, sometimes nonsensical, perception of reality, and reaffirm our commitment to relaxation, doing this with gratitude and joy.

As we bring a sense of relaxation to any and every situation, we consciously embrace a new way of travelling, with faith, ease and grace at the helm. We begin to allow the proverbial ship of life to sail herself as we relish every port and vista, with true inner peace as our ever-faithful companion.

AFFIRMATIONS

Stressing is an option, not a necessity.
I embrace a calm life.

As I let go and flow with life, life becomes ever
gentler and easier for me.

My peaceful thoughts are always heard
and echoed by the universe.

JOURNAL PROMPTS

I now choose to live a peaceful life because ...

I notice myself releasing tension when ...

As I choose to relax into a calmer way of life, I let go of ...

PRAYER

May calmness embrace me as I open my
heart and mind to peaceful thoughts,
ease and grace.

As I trust more deeply in the way things
naturally are, I allow myself to flow
forward in perfect rhythm, time and
space. I choose to relax, rest well
and soften into life with full faith.

AUTHENTICITY
AND BLISS

One of my favourite wisdoms around relaxation is the
Chinese proverb 'Tension is who you think you should
be, relaxation is who you are.' All too often, we have
redundant, preconceived ideas about how our lives
should look. How we should look. How things should be.
It is prudent for us to become very attuned to the word
'should' as it suggests rifts between our thoughts,
feelings and actions. When we become aware of our
personal use of the word 'should' in daily life, we can
flag it, becoming more curious about how it feels. We
can use these 'should' moments to ask ourselves very
good questions that help us better understand our
thoughts and feelings. We can notice the areas of our
lives in which we are abandoning or compromising
our true selves to be something or someone we're not.

Profound, timeless and pure relaxation is found in the experience
of being our authentic selves. This kind of bliss involves choosing
not to withhold our essential natures, passions, beliefs and creativity,
even our eccentricity, from ourselves and others. It involves finding
beauty in the little things about ourselves that make us so special
and unique as individuals.

In the story of Alice in Wonderland, the Mad Hatter asks Alice if she thinks he has gone mad. She delightfully replies:

'I'm afraid so.
You're entirely bonkers.
But I will tell you a secret,
all the best people are!'

When we refresh our perspective and approve of ourselves, we can experience being loved just as we are. Indeed, awakened self-approval is a wonderful elixir for lasting relaxation and inner peace. If we live consciously with love and respect for ourselves and others, there are no parts of us that need to be neatened or censored so as to become more likeable to others. We must be mindful that those who love and appreciate us just as we are will be those with whom we truly wish to share our lives. It is also comforting to realise that while certain relationships are forever, others are for particular times and places, seasons and reasons in our lives.

As we grow and change in alignment with our values and essence, we may notice that we move in different directions from people with whom we no longer feel so resonant. In respect for our personal growth, and in acceptance of the inevitability of change, we may gently free ourselves and others to pursue paths of truth and integrity. Such profound trust in ourselves and life liberates us to experience deep relaxation. It supports us to circumnavigate the exhaustion of drama, the pain of unmet expectations and the tension of holding on to things at our own expense.

It is very stressful to be untrue to ourselves and to act in ways that are contrary to our values, beliefs and spirits - to abandon ourselves when the infinite wellspring of joy we seek is right at home within us. It is very un-relaxing to disapprove of and judge ourselves, just as it is to disapprove of and judge others with whom we share our lives.

The best way to evolve beyond negativity and exhaustion in this regard is to adopt a 'live and let live' mentality. A live and let live mentality allows ourselves and others to be as we are and enjoy our lives in freedom and peace. As we settle into a more relaxed way of being, we extend peace well beyond ourselves. In the words of the poet Atticus,

'Watch carefully the magic that occurs when you give a person just enough comfort to be themselves.'

As we learn to relax, we are gifted with greater mental, physical and emotional agility. The Dalai Lama teaches that an open heart is an open mind. The more relaxed, open and flexible we are, the more joyous, spontaneous and enchanting our lives become. When we are harmonious, relaxed and at ease with ourselves and life, we move like beautiful willow trees, bending and swaying when the winds of change blow. By contrast, when we are rigid and inflexible, when we resist ourselves, resist the magic of life and defy the inevitability of constant change, we are very unlikely to bend gracefully and much more likely to break. Relying on our moral compass to guide us into the territory of higher values, including compassion, tolerance and kindness, we can continue to open our hearts over time, expanding our minds, healing our bodies and fortifying our spirits.

As we lovingly accept and celebrate ourselves, our view of others with whom we share our world softens and expands. We experience greater lightness, patience and satisfaction, and the gentler, more loving perspective we cultivate within us positively colours our experience of life. Just as happiness is said to be an inside job, so is relaxation. All that we need to know about relaxation dwells within us. Our role, quite simply, is to open our hearts and minds to the freedom we seek.

AFFIRMATIONS

As I open my heart and mind, relaxation comes to me easily.

Tension is who I think I should be, relaxation is who I am.

Freedom to be myself is my lifelong gift.

JOURNAL PROMPTS

I am true to myself when I ...

Some of my most unusual or interesting personal qualities include ...

I would find life flowed more easily if I could be more open-minded about ...

PRAYER

With this prayer I lovingly accept and celebrate myself.

I drop the need to perform or impress, and release the desire to be anyone other than who I truly am. In my realness, I come home.

I express thanks for the wonderful people in my life who love me for who I am, and welcome new ways of seeing and experiencing my true essence.

Being authentic, I feel joy return to my heart and calmness to my mind. All tension melts away as I find my own bliss, my spirit deeply at peace.

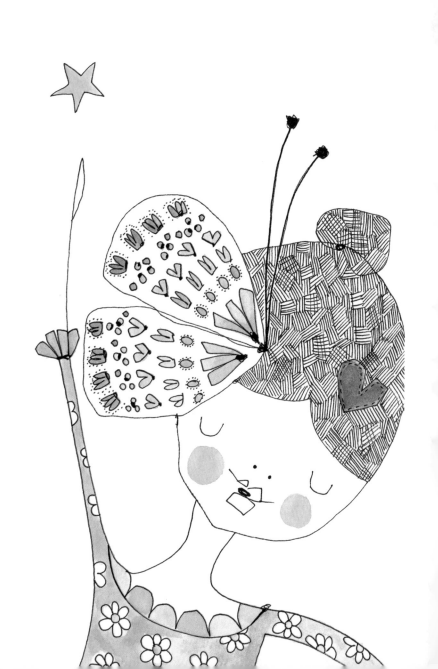

LIGHTNESS AND
GOOD HUMOUR

Our lives become easier, more relaxing and much more
fun when we embrace good humour and savour the
lightness of being. Choosing to smile, laugh and play
more in daily life nurtures our wellbeing, expands
our creativity and nourishes our relationships with
ourselves and others. A sense of humour elevates our
communication and makes us more relatable to others.
Becoming too serious at our own and others' expense
stiffens us to life and causes unnecessary tension.
With rigid filters of perception, we lose our perspective,
diminishing the joy and delight life freely offers us.
Maturing doesn't mean that our sense of wonder,
curiosity and cheekiness need to dwindle. It was
Plato, in his timeless wisdom, who suggested that
life should be lived as play.

Lightness and good humour are healthy and relaxing virtues to cultivate, as joy strengthens us at the cellular level. Joy supports all the workings of our bodies, including our immunity, and fortifies us for long and happy lives. Laughter therapy is a form of therapy enjoyed the world over, where participants are quite simply encouraged to laugh out loud. At the very beginning, the laughter is 'on cue', but from one giggle to the next, real laughter and real joy begin to flow.

Similarly, Smiling Therapy relaxes all the muscles in our faces and allows them to feel peace at last.

A tight jaw and a furrowed brow can melt into the experience of a smile. We can try this right now, simply by softening our eyes, our cheeks, our lips and our teeth, allowing ourselves to create a smile, very gently. We can close our eyes at this point, immersing ourselves in the feeling. Again, slowly but surely, this smile we create with effort becomes a more natural smile. The messages we send our minds, bodies and spirits when we laugh, smile and play help us to relax and truly enjoy our lives.

As well as offering wellbeing benefits, there are other practical
advantages in cultivating lightness and good humour. Former US
president Dwight Eisenhower commented that 'a sense of humor
is part of the art of leadership, of getting along with people, of
getting things done.' Indeed, humour is a very well-understood,
international language. Even when words fail us, a laugh or smile
can speak volumes, breaking the proverbial ice, diffusing tension
and opening doors to heartfelt connection. Good humour is an
expression of our warmth and intelligence, of our willingness to
form meaningful bonds with others. It is an assertion that life is to
be relished, critiqued with a delicious sense of wit, savoured with
a sharpening of our faculties and enjoyed with a spring in our step.

Loosening our fixed-thought processes and ways of seeing things allows us to rise up and take a bird's-eye view upon our circumstances, assisting us to see them in context and offering us valuable perspective and peace.

The famous words of the old rhyme 'Row, row, row your boat, gently down the stream … Merrily, merrily, merrily, merrily, life is but a dream' ring powerfully true. Acknowledging the sanctity of life and the gravitas of the responsibility and privilege of being alive is best done with an acute sense of the oftentimes sheer absurdity of living. The ever-present, inexplicable mystery of life.

Laughing in what could be considered inappropriate circumstances may also be enjoyed as part of embracing our humanity. Certain things cannot be made sense of, but with humour and lightness we discover inroads to appreciation and grace. Indeed, life is but a dream and, as the naturalist Thoreau reminds us, our truest lives are when we are in dreams awake.

Lightness and good humour help to centre us when we feel off balance and they assist us to identify the ever-present 'silver linings', some of which simply take a few moments more to see in the face of adversity. Choosing good humour gifts us with much-needed little boosts of positive energy to uplift and sustain us throughout our days, reminding us not to take ourselves or our lives too seriously. Things we may see as terribly important can in retrospect fade into the greater fabric of life.

Paying too much intense attention to things does not support our attempts to relax. In the lovely words of philosopher William James: 'Common sense and a sense of humour are the same thing moving at different speeds. A sense of humour is just common sense, dancing.' We have a choice to relax by seeing and experiencing life with lightness and good humour. Awakening each morning to recognise and harness this choice is a gift to ourselves and all others with whom we share the play of life.

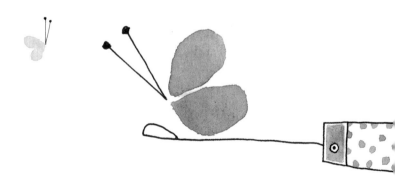

AFFIRMATIONS

Life is a joy when I'm having fun.

I consciously choose lightness as
I cultivate peace.

My spirit sparkles with cheekiness and play.

JOURNAL PROMPTS

I feel a sense of lightness and joy when ...

My sense of humour would be helpful
in situations such as ...

My cheekiest pleasures include ...

PRAYER

With this prayer I ask that my spirit be
touched by lightness and peace.

May I always find paths to perspective,
laughter and joy, even in the face of
adversity.

May the exquisite vibrancy and cheekiness
within me be fully expressed in loving company,
and may my creativity expand as
I embrace the magic of life.

RELAXING
COMMUNICATION

The way we communicate in the world — the way
we translate our thoughts into speech and move our
bodies through space — becomes more peaceful and
beautiful when we choose relaxation as a way of life.
Communicating in a relaxed way with ourselves and
others, and choosing gentler touch, slower movement and
a less hurried pace of living creates the spaciousness
and pleasure we seek. As we relax, situations that would
once vex and overwhelm us become more approachable.

Peaceful energy emanates from us, calming the
personal atmosphere in which we move through life and
facilitating smoother interactions of all kinds. While the
busy world around us may toss and turn, we can choose
to embrace life within the proverbial eye of the storm,
feeling solid, composed and attuned to bliss.

We truly underestimate the power and influence of our chosen thoughts and words, particularly stressful words deriving from stressful thoughts. Developing a kinder, more conscious way of communicating with ourselves and others is a life-changing choice, as our thoughts and words shape our realities. We don't see things as they are; we see things as we are. Expressions such as I can't stand this, I don't have time, I'm dying of hunger, this is killing me, I'm just too busy, things never work out, this drives me crazy, and so on, add unnecessary drama and complication to our experience of life.

These seemingly innocuous but profoundly unsettling turns of phrase have become a part of common vernacular at our great expense. Our subconscious minds have no sense of humour and, as a result, believe the thoughts we choose to think and the words we choose to speak. Without actively intercepting stressful thoughts and dramatic speech, we can slowly but surely come to exist in a pool of negative, tiring and unsupportive energy. No wonder we can feel unsettled, that our sense of wellbeing is diminished and that life is very hard for us. By contrast, positive and mindful thoughts and words soothe and inspire us.

I can handle this,

I have time for all the things I wish to enjoy,

I nourish myself all throughout the day,

life is always on my side,

this is tricky but with a little time,

I'll get there.

We need only take a moment to feel the extraordinary energy
that calmer, kinder, more empowering words and ideas generate.
Take a moment now to feel the extraordinary energy of calmer,
kinder words.

We are wise to awaken to the power of gentler thinking. We can
all nurture peaceful and productive minds by interrupting unhelpful
thoughts as they emerge. We intuitively know that over-complicated,
worrisome and dramatic thoughts cause us stress and thieve our joy.
Yet, when we begin to interact with our thoughts as choices, we
are empowered. We see that stressful thoughts are not only
unhelpful and unnecessary, they are also illusory, flexible and
completely transformable.

As we relax, it becomes easier to recognise and refine agitating thoughts. Rather than punishing ourselves for creating and indulging stress, we can simply smile and congratulate ourselves as we interrupt unhelpful thoughts, one by one. The more we self-correct tense thoughts with simpler, more peaceful ones, the gentler, smoother and more joyous our lives naturally become.

Bringing time and care to our thoughts brings greater finesse and meaning to the words we speak. In simplifying our speech, we say what we mean and mean what we say. At peace, we are able to speak more clearly, honestly and kindly. Sensitivity and directness in speech instils our interpersonal exchanges with clarity and ease. Rather than thinking, speaking and acting in stressed, circuitous ways that can leave us feeling anxious and misunderstood by others, we can simplify our lives to gain the time and space to truly know ourselves. This affords us the clarity and confidence to express our minds and hearts aloud.

While difficult situations are part and parcel of the fabric of life, we do not need to be stressed. While stress and busyness bring a sense of self-importance, success or satisfaction to some, any inroad to fulfilment through tension is very taxing on the spirit. It is not an essential part of our human experience to be terribly busy and perpetually stressed. We needn't move our bodies with unnecessary rush, nor think and speak in tense, hurried ways, nor subscribe to stress, existing in restlessness. Each day, we can choose differently, and choose peace and wellbeing. Indeed, releasing our fixed notions of stress as normal or inevitable opens up possibilities for living that we might have previously thought implausible.

Through mindful and relaxing
communication we can embody and
share our peace in infinite ways that
help to soften and enhance our
everyday experiences.

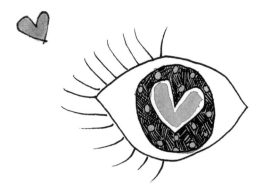

Bringing conscious thoughts into conscious speech and action creates a climate of trust, confidence and peace within and around us. As we encourage ourselves to feel peaceful and safe through choosing relaxation, others may feel safe and calm in our presence.

Our body language also calls for attention and care, as our bodies always speak our minds. Whether we realise it or not, we say so much with our tone of voice and our gaze, the way we move our hands and the way we hold and carry ourselves. We can bring greater bliss and joy to our lives and the lives of others quite simply by attending to our unique, personal language in any moment.

We can replace a stark glare with a soft gaze, a harsh tone of speech with a gentler one and crossed arms and furrowed brows with more open stances and expressions, and upgrade from emotional absence to careful listening. Rather than moving through space absent-minded, hurried and heavy-handed, we can embrace lightness of touch and being. Learning to bring our relaxed and mindful presence to each and every moment, we may flourish each day as moving prayers of peace.

AFFIRMATIONS

I take loving responsibility for cultivating
positive energy within and around me.

Calming thoughts relax and nourish me.

I am empowered by calm communication.

JOURNAL PROMPTS

I now become more aware of my
self-talk in these areas ...

Reflecting on my personal body language,
I notice ...

In my communications with others,
I can cultivate peace by ...

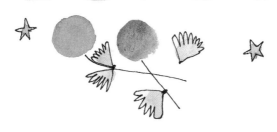

PRAYER

Each moment, I have the option to express myself in loving, compassionate, kind and creative ways that honour myself and those with whom I share my world.

May I be gifted with all the patience, courage and strength I need now as I choose to live my life in peace.

THE CALMING
EFFECT OF
SIMPLICITY

There is magnificence in simplicity. A single
flower in a glass vase. Thoughtful economy of
phrase. A simple meal made with fresh produce and
love. A clean room brimming with natural light.
One heavenly brushstroke on a page.

We have the option to bring the grace and beauty
of simplicity to each moment we have: to all that
we think, say and do. A deeply relaxing way of
life reveals itself to us as we consciously declutter
our busy thoughts and ideas, spaces and schedules.
Through the spaciousness, freedom and peace of
simpler living, we may savour the beauty of life
with profound attention to detail.

When we simplify our thoughts, we simplify our lives. Our minds have a habit of compounding matters. We speculate about what could or should happen in the future and dwell in the past. We disenchant ourselves with unrealistic expectations and, in our very busy ways of living, pass right by the present moments we have. As we learn to relax, it becomes easier to declutter and streamline our thoughts and realities. This is a joyous and life-changing process.

We can embrace simplicity in daily life by arranging more relaxed itineraries that, while stimulating and productive, allow us time to rest, relax and pursue pleasures that truly inspire us. Jam-packing our days can cause us to feel overwhelmed. While we think we achieve a great deal when rushing and racing, downtime and rest exponentially improve the quality of our lives and our efforts in all areas.

We can hardly enjoy our activities, nor acknowledge and celebrate our various achievements, when we pack our days to the very brim without reflection and reprieve.

Rather than racing from thing to thing and place to place, we can actively simplify our schedules for greater health, harmony and happiness.

Allowing breathing space in our daily lives for the deliciousness
of spontaneity and free time imbues us with greater energy and
wellbeing for embracing life. Being still allows butterflies of joy and
beauty to alight upon us, inspiring our creativity. Contrary to stifling
and outmoded beliefs about achieving productivity through stressful,
relentless toil, we may find that by choosing relaxation we positively
harness and revolutionise every opportunity, connection and
moment we have. We quite simply come to savour more expressive,
exquisite and enriching lives.

Choice is a great privilege we often take for granted, though in many instances we are positively spoilt for it.

We simply have too many things to choose from in our daily lives … and end up depleted by decision fatigue. We can have wardrobes overflowing with clothes yet feel we have nothing to wear. We can have pantries and fridges full of ingredients yet nothing to eat. We can accrue countless possessions for the thrill of purchasing and having them, though they are not needed and clutter our homes and our lives. Decluttering our possessions and our spaces allows us to experience the great joy of relaxation.

When we have only what we need and
truly love around us, avoiding gratuitous
excess, we have less to think about and
more time, space and richness to enjoy.

Mindfully kept spaces and a meaningful, minimal collection of personal possessions are signs of gratitude, restraint and respect. When standing in a thoughtfully composed, uncluttered interior or garden, or when standing in front of an ordered desk or clean cupboard, it is no surprise that we notice a sense of relaxation touch us.

There is truth to the old adage that simple is best. A home-cooked meal made with love can bring us more comfort and pleasure than a lavish dinner out. A handful of carefully foraged blooms can say more than a fancy bouquet. A few kind, honest words and the touch of a hand can bring more peace than an elaborate apology. While the words 'simple' and 'easy' are often used interchangeably, they are mutually exclusive. Simple isn't easy. Consciously choosing simplicity in a busy material world requires mindful attention and care – but if we seek to live relaxing and joyous lives, it is well worth the effort.

AFFIRMATIONS

I embrace simplicity to soothe my spirit.

I relax my busy schedule to create
time and space for joy.

I savour limitless beauty through
mindful living.

JOURNAL PROMPTS

This example of simplicity brings me joy ...

I look forward to decluttering these
parts of my life ...

I need less ...
and more ...

PRAYER

With this prayer I acknowledge the beauty,
ease and grace of simplicity in my life.

I now go forward unencumbered by clutter, and
in a spirit of gratitude and peace.

As I choose to live simply, honestly and richly,
my happiness grows.

I thank life wholeheartedly for gifting me the
things that matter most.

NOURISHING
FOUNDATIONS
FOR DEEP
RELAXATION

When our minds and bodies are relaxed, deeply
nourished and humming, our spirits can express
their inherent vibrancy and vitality. Wholefoods,
deep sleep, uplifting movement and nurturing
self-care rituals have profoundly positive impacts
on our wellbeing. By virtue of loving self-care,
we can support our minds and bodies to find
pathways to relaxation and wellbeing in daily life.

What is deeply relaxing for one person may not be so blissful for another. For those who love touch, the idea of a massage can bring instant relief. For others, reading a book in a quiet space might offer more peace and comfort. The pleasure of moving will bring greater relaxation to some than the thought of stillness. A walk in nature may be preferred over a long, decadent candlelit bath. A gentle movie over meditation. What relaxes us as individuals is a celebration of our uniqueness, and a true pleasure to explore.

As we attune ourselves to the essence of relaxation in moments of peace, we learn to sense our minds and bodies at ease. We feel our muscles, thoughts and breath soften. We might sense a lightness of being, feel our self-consciousness melting away, notice a positive perspective returning, and feel the energy of inspiration move us. We might even sense an expanded state of awareness grace our minds as we access meditative states of flow, losing track of time and space for a while as we drop down from our busy minds into our feeling hearts.

Recognising these peaceful feelings within us, we learn to discover and collect experiences that relax us. All we must then do to bring greater peace and calm into our days is commit to prioritising and freely enjoying the divine things that soothe and nourish us.

Above and beyond our individual pleasures, as delightful and varied as we are, the rudimentary foundations of nourishment for relaxation are universal, including real food, deep rest and peaceful shelter. Mindfully chosen and consciously savoured edible nourishment strengthens and relaxes our minds and bodies. Rather than ride the fickle waves of sugar, caffeine and processed non-foods each day, we can choose a whole-food, nutrient-rich diet of plant-based foods from Mother Earth. Eating consciously, we needn't experience the unwanted slumps in energy and mood we might have come to accept as part and parcel of 'stressful' modern life. We can quite simply choose differently and, in doing so, live differently.

We cannot underestimate how critical good nourishment is for the maintenance of healthy nervous systems, minds and bodies.

By eating real food at regular intervals, and not skipping meals or substituting vacuous non-foods for true nourishment, we find ourselves feeling steady, clear-headed, energised and relaxed. Being part of the natural world, our human bodies understand what is whole and real. In harnessing the tremendous energy of the natural world through healing wholefoods, we foster a climate of gratitude and vitality within us. We satiate ourselves for life and build reservoirs of resilience and peace.

Resting our bodies with deep sleep and regular downtime calms and energises us. When we are rested and relaxed, we find that 'being' more and 'doing' less is a conscious choice for deep fulfilment and aliveness. If we struggle to switch off and relax, we can seek out ways to soothe and settle ourselves with natural medicines, herbs, essential oils, yogic stretches or gentle music to support our relaxation.

Lemon balm tea before bed, a dash of lavender essential oil on our pillowslip, quiet, meditative music, even transposing our thoughts into words through journal-keeping, all help to encourage and welcome deep rest. Kindness towards ourselves as we learn to relax is essential. As with any profound and aspirational change we seek to bring into our lives, time, care, patience and commitment are required. Go gently. Rest comes naturally to us all when we choose relaxation. Moving our bodies heals, strengthens and enlivens us.

Stiff, inflexible bodies create climates for rigid, inflexible minds, while bodies stretched by movement and exploration expand into bright new dimensions. Enjoy the many wonderful things your body can do. Allow the energy of life to flow through you as you walk, swim, stretch, dance and enjoy any form of movement you please. Let the mind–body benefits of exercise bring greater peace and bliss into your everyday life.

Taking shelter in a relaxing environment gifts us with true solace, comfort and delight. With loving attention, our homes can become our personalised sanctuaries of relaxation. Consider choosing gentle colours to furnish your surroundings, embrace natural light and air, play soothing music, arrange fresh flowers and maintain clean and clear interior spaces that encourage deeper relaxation.

The time and care you take to nurture your home
with love will nourish you very deeply in return.
Indeed, the world we create around us reflects the
world we nurture within us. As we relax at home
within, the outer spaces in which we take shelter,
live and breathe may become beautiful, interactive
expressions of our inner peace.

AFFIRMATIONS

I nourish myself naturally with love, time and care.

I sense when my mind and body are at ease.

My wellbeing flourishes when I relax.

JOURNAL PROMPTS

I presently nurture my wellbeing (mind, body and spirit) in these ways ...

I can actively create beautiful and inspiring spaces around me by ...

Moving calmly ahead, I look forward to caring for myself in these extra ways ...

PRAYER

Thank you, Life, for nourishing
me deeply with beauty, joy, mystery
and inspiration.

I am truly thankful for the bounty
of this earth and my own harmony
within the symphony of life.

May the food I eat, the rest I enjoy,
the love I show myself, and the shelter
I take soothe my spirit and fulfil
me completely.

MINDFULNESS,
MOVEMENT
AND BREATH

Breathing deeply in a hurried world is true
mindfulness in motion. Actively slowing down
to rest, move gently, breathe fully and ground
our personal energy rewards us with a range
of remarkably relaxing benefits. Mindful living,
moving and breathing offer us greater mental
and physical flexibility, deeper peace of mind,
a refreshed perspective for positive thinking and
decision making, and the gift of being awake
and aware in the present moment: the most
precious moment we have.

Writer Etty Hillesum asserted that the most important moment of the day is the space between two deep breaths. Indeed, directing our awareness to the fact that we are breathing catapults us right back into the here and now, assisting us to connect our busy thinking minds with our living, breathing physical bodies.

As we connect our minds and bodies through breath awareness, we are less likely to feel breathless, hurried or compromised as we go about our lives. Indeed, when we reconnect with our breath, we reconnect with ourselves, accessing the light, space and air we seek.

When we disconnect from our breath and allow the constant motion of life to distract us from ourselves and what truly matters, it is very hard to feel satisfied and relaxed.

Unconscious, rushed living, or existence on autopilot due to apathy or sheer exhaustion, offers very little in the way of peace and joy. Truly living involves being aware of ourselves, of those with whom we share our lives and of the earth herself: the rhythms of day and night, the majestic beauty of the natural world with which we are called to live in harmony and the lessons taught to us by nature, including patience, resilience and imperfect perfection. Just as the earth lives and breathes, so do we.

Enjoying activities that connect our minds and bodies supports us to enjoy calmer, more relaxed and balanced lives. Forms of mindfulness in motion that involve linking movement with breath include yoga and Pilates, tai chi and qigong, even mindful walking and meditative dance. Relaxing our bodies with conscious movement relaxes our minds, just as relaxing our minds soothes our bodies. Indeed, greater agility in the body speaks to greater agility in the mind and vice versa. Becoming more curious about the significance and power of this moment-to-moment interconnection can help to pique our interest in, and our respect for, harmonising our mind–body.

Sufi mystic Rumi encourages us to move beyond our thoughts so
that we may drink the nectar of the present moment. If we catch
ourselves being overwhelmed by thoughts, forgetting to breathe
and suddenly feeling quite stressed, we can simply hear the words
'breathe in, breathe out' within us, or, if we feel moved to, we can
speak them gently aloud. Breathing in and out, we let cleansing air
purify and refresh our bodies. We let go of the old and welcome
the new. Indeed, breathing is a deeply healing, detoxifying natural
wonder. Our breath is our life force and is a lifelong pleasure to
explore. Breathing is a moment-to-moment relationship with
ourselves and life. It is the very beginning, very essence and
very end of our earthly adventures. Each moment we breathe,
we are gifted with life.

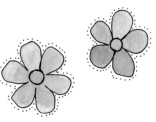

Mindful living is awakened living in which
we live in gratitude and harmony with all
that we have and all that we are.

When we move through life unaware of the profound blessings
all around us, blessings that are ours to enjoy, we miss so many
opportunities to grow our happiness, wisdom and peace. In the
flow of life in which we feel part of a greater whole, we are able
to settle into a knowingness of things being just so: just as night
follows day and our out-breath follows our in-breath.

Awareness of our breath connects us with the divine order of
the universe and, with our loving attention, can imbue us with a
profound sense of belonging and aliveness, and the preciousness of
the present moment. The past is over and the future is yet to come.
The present moment is the only moment we truly have. Breathing
gently in and gently out, placing hands upon our hearts, we may
express simple little prayers of gratitude that delight, elevate and
relax us in daily life.

Being mindful of our earth, we notice the beauty of our natural
world. We appreciate light, space, air and shadows: the infinite
colours, textures and forms of things. Being conscious of our minds,
we appreciate our creativity and wisdom, and our interconnection
with all life. Being mindful of our bodies, we savour and celebrate
our aliveness, and being mindful in our relationships, we may bring
deeper love and understanding to those with whom we share our
lives. Being mindful, we relax.

AFFIRMATIONS

I choose to move flowingly
and breathe deeply.

I live in gratitude for all that
I have and all that I am.

My mind and body flourish in harmony.

JOURNAL PROMPTS

I feel very present and alive when ...

As I pay closer attention to
my breathing, I notice ...

I look forward to exploring
more mindful living by ...

PRAYER

With this prayer I honour my sacred body:
all its lines and shapes, and all the
wonderful things it can do.

As I nourish myself with mindfulness, movement
and breath, I feel my spirit come alive.

May I grow stronger and feel calmer
each day, experiencing my life as a rich,
enchanting pleasure.

RELAXATION,
PRODUCTIVITY
AND SUCCESS

Rest, quiet time, an early night snuggled up on the sofa with a good book, a cup of tea in bed – delicious moments of peace and calm such as these relax and refresh our minds, bodies and spirits. When rested and relaxed, we are able to engage our faculties to the fullest: to access the richness of our creativity, enjoy greater energy and physical flexibility, and experience true clarity and crispness of mind. If we push ourselves relentlessly, we ignore vital cues to slow down. Forgoing rest for fear of feeling lazy and unproductive, or being confronted with the reality of our thoughts and feelings in the quiet of our own company, we sabotage our wellness and peace. Honouring our need to relax in daily life helps us manage our priorities, find balance and enjoy a sense of peace and calm.

The brilliant design of our minds remains unchanged from days gone by in which we had far less stimulation to process and manage in daily life. It is no wonder that if we don't keep our wits about us, the sensory overload of modern living can tug at our peace and joy. In times past, we human beings would have lived far more simply, tending to our immediate needs in greater harmony with nature. We were surrounded by less infrastructure, had fewer choices and relied on verbal storytelling, art and dance to accrue wisdom and information. We lived in interdependent communities, and their collective spirit was a determining factor for our vitality and survival.

Today we receive endless alerts from our devices as we rush through our days. We are ever-available to others by virtue of technology and, while we are more 'connected' than ever before, many of us feel separate and lonely, navigating life between our material and virtual worlds.

In pursuit of balance, we squeeze into our jam-packed agendas good nutrition, exercise, hobbies, time at work and time with friends, and, if we can possibly manage, we incorporate some kind of altruistic, loving service.

Somewhere in between all these activities might enter the subtlest, most profound call to slow down, rest and relax. Yet amid all the doing, just being might seem impossible – something we need to save until later. The beautiful Zen proverb suggesting that the best time to relax is when we don't have time can open our eyes to the possibility of living quite differently.

We may aspire to involve ourselves in life to the fullest, yet we needn't arrive at the finishing lines of our days and lives feeling breathless and overwrought. We needn't look back and see that in our busyness we missed ourselves, life and the ones we loved. Equipping ourselves with sustaining, fortifying calmness through daily rest and relaxation supports us to face challenges with grace, reach positive solutions and disprove ideologies equating success with incessant productivity. Indeed, stillness and rest are intelligent forms of self-care that gives us the charge we need for better living.

The poet Ovid beautifully wrote that 'a rested field yields a bountiful crop'. It is just so for us human beings.

We have normalised, even glorified, busyness at our great expense — so much so that when we are not busy we can feel unsuccessful, idle or guilty. We fear that things might fall apart if we drop the proverbial ball of life to rest and dip out of the race — and yet, for most of us, the possibility of letting go, attempting a new way of being and exploring fresh possibilities for living is mysterious and beautiful. With greater integrity and faith in life, we may live in alignment with our values, and watch life rise to meet us in our lives and dreams. The dreamers among us who choose to subvert rushing trends, to live more slowly, possibly more sparingly and certainly more imaginatively, may set precedents for others who are awakening to the power of rest, relaxation and peace in daily life.

Let us take regular time out to relax and daydream, take simple holidays and spend time in nature. Let us unplug from our devices whenever and wherever possible, treating ourselves with tenderness as human beings rather than busy, unbreakable machines of a modern era. Let us rest when we are tired or unwell rather than silence and mask our intuitive wisdom with dismissive quick fixes. Let us reclaim and nurture our independence, creativity and intelligence by relying more on ourselves.

Let us share meaningfully in community. Let us exercise gently and lovingly to nourish ourselves rather than punish our bodies into submission with intense regimes. Let us enjoy early nights, comfy sheets and gentle moments with ourselves and others. Let us take peaceful time to know, love and be with ourselves so that we may be part of pioneering new, healthier, more balanced ways of being that energise us at a spiritual level for truly wonderful and fulfilling lives.

AFFIRMATIONS

I savour the pleasures of work,
rest and play.

I find daily happiness in mindful balance.

I fully allow myself to rest and relax.

JOURNAL PROMPTS

I feel most balanced and
at peace when ...

I could slow down in these areas
of my life ...

My favourite ways to rest
and relax include ...

PRAYER

With this prayer, I welcome rest and
relaxation into my life.

I respectfully acknowledge the calls
of my mind, body and spirit as I consciously
slow down to embrace and enjoy each new day.

I ask for support as I live mindfully,
finding calm and clear ways to balance work,
rest and play.

I settle into myself in quiet moments of bliss,
knowing that I am at home within, and trusting
in the comfort of my own love and care.

CREATING

HEAVEN

ON EARTH

The world in which we live asks us to hold what is magical, mysterious and miraculous in the same hand as that which seems to be rational, reasonable and logical. Our daily life is a spellbinding combination of things heavenly and ethereal, material and earthly. We live in a world of things seen and unseen, of feelings deeply felt. In a time and place in which we face great challenges personally, interpersonally and environmentally, in which the temperature of our planet and the internal climate of humanity is rising, it is no wonder that we can become hardened, cynical and doubtful when pondering the possibility of divine healing and intervention — of creating and enjoying heaven on earth. Yet there could be nothing more life-affirming, necessary and inspirational than suspending our disbelief, softening into the potential for tremendous transformation and allowing ourselves to envision a harmonious, sublime new present and future.

Nourishing our inner peace through relaxation gifts us with a calmer, lighter and more joyous lens through which to view life and living. As we cultivate a more peaceful, appreciative attitude within ourselves, we may bring greater optimism and creativity to daily life. Taking care of our personal wellness in this way, we support our minds, bodies and spirits to explore new territory. We begin to dream beyond our present moment, welcoming new courage and inspiration as we embark upon fresh adventures. We expand our endeavours beyond that which we already see and know.

What if our lives could look and feel completely refreshed? And what if we were to see well beyond ourselves as individuals and view ourselves as integral parts of a unified whole? What if we could come together one by one, day by day, choosing community, collaboration and unity over clutching and competitiveness? How changed our world would be.

That we see ourselves as very different from and separate to one
another is a futile, devastating and outworn construct. It stems
from our spiritual disconnection from the oneness of life. Differing
race, creed, culture, sex, politics and points of view are essential to
the texture and diversity of life on earth. We are here to grow and
learn from one another – to see, touch, feel and sense vividly – to
experience the richness of life. Beneath our external differences
pulsates our shared humanity – our collective spirit – woven
from the earthly and heavenly threads that bind us. To spend just
a moment harnessing the power of our oneness is to embrace the
possibility of heaven on earth.

When we take personal responsibility for choosing relaxation and loving kindness, we become part of a healing wave of peace on earth. We begin to positively alter the atmosphere within and around us, contributing to greater calmness and vitality.

While we may sometimes feel that what we perceive as our small contribution means little in the face of a big world needing change, we are wise to remember that if we all felt this way, powerless and incapable of making a positive difference, no real change would ever be made. One person can change a day, change a life and change the world. We are more powerful than we choose to realise, and our conscious, loving presence on this earth truly matters.

If we wish to be part of creating heaven on earth we must begin by believing in the possibility of it. Relaxing and tuning into the power of love helps fortify us to believe in miracles and embrace the magic of life.

We must also connect with our personal power, thinking, speaking and acting in ways that bring ourselves, others and our earth greater peace and joy. Next we must project for a tranquil and heavenly world by holding a splendid picture of earthly bliss in our hearts and minds, even manifesting for peace and calm during our daydreams, meditations and prayers. This active practice can be gentle or ecstatic: a quiet note to the universe or a resplendent dance of bliss.

How we choose to create or express heaven on earth is our divine pleasure to explore. As we choose to live calmer and more peaceful lives, we awaken to loving energy within and around us. Ensconced in a climate of love, we begin to feel embraced by a sense of belonging – a relaxing and enriching sense of oneness. Living mindfully day by day, the beauty and energy of life can inspire and fortify us, restoring faith in ourselves and in the exquisite possibility of heavenly life on earth.

AFFIRMATIONS

I take part in creating heaven on earth.

I sense my oneness with others.

I embrace all possibilities for peace.

JOURNAL PROMPTS

To me,
heaven on earth would look like ...

To me,
heaven on earth would feel like ...

I can actively take part in cultivating
heaven on earth by ...

PRAYER

Heaven, help me to believe in peace and harmony on earth.

Even when I am most challenged by that which lies before me, strengthen my faith in the beauty, perfection and magic of life.

As I choose to live calmly in a spirit of love, help me to shine brightly as a light with and for others.

May I actively contribute to peace on earth, blissfully at one with myself and all creation.

To choose relaxation, to make time for it, savour and appreciate it, is a gift to ourselves and to all those with whom we enjoy our lives. As relaxation nourishes and strengthens us, we feel more vital and inspired. We feel energised to share our unique gifts each day, enhancing our relationships, our creativity and our complete wellbeing.

Allowing relaxation to support us physically, mentally and emotionally means actively slowing down to live in gentler, more conscious ways. It also involves finding ease and grace by leading authentic lives true to our ourselves: our values, essences and dreams. As we begin to relax, we come to see and communicate with greater clarity. We breathe more deeply, delight in the levity of good humour and savour the joy of daily delights great and small.

Choosing relaxation allows us to feel touched by the soothing benefits of simplicity. In creating simpler, calmer lives, we learn to compassionately untangle unhelpful, knotty thoughts, words and actions. We make space for quietness and bliss each day, allowing our lives to flow with less tension and more joy.

Choosing to build and nurture peaceful lives is always our choice, even in the face of inevitable adversity and challenge. Indeed, equipping ourselves with practical tools for relaxation in our self-care repertoire helps us to build resilience in daily life. By balancing our work, rest and play in more self-caring ways, we come to experience deep inner peace, fulfilment and calm.

By choosing relaxation for ourselves and sharing our peaceful personal energy with others as we move about our lives, we partake in creating heaven on earth: a reality in which we may all experience greater freedom, gratitude and joy. Let us choose relaxation and, in doing so, feel imbued with fresh energy and inspiration as we walk meaningful paths through this miraculous life.

ACKNOWLEDGEMENTS

This peaceful little book has been brought to life with the loving support of my publisher, Hardie Grant. A special thanks to Sandy Grant and Pam Brewster. I appreciate your faith in me. A heartfelt thank you to book designer Mietta Yans for making these pages especially beautiful, and to Allison Hiew for her gentle and thoughtful editing. Thank you to Joanna Wong for her project management and to Todd Rechner for overseeing the fine details of this book's production.

Thank you to Mick Smith and his team at Splitting Image, and to graphic artist Meaghan Thomson for the careful handling of my original artworks in ink and watercolour. Thank you to Jane Grant for her work behind the scenes, and to my generous confidant and dear friend Fiona Lang for her invaluable time and care. Thank you Kirstie Grant for managing the publicity of this and my other titles, to book retailers and representatives around Australia and overseas, and to passionate, caring book lovers around the world.

Thank you to my parents Roslyn and Michael Gaston, and to my beloved grandparents and ancestors in spirit for their continued inspiration and support. Thank you to my loved ones and friends, you know who you are. You bring so much happiness and richness to my life.

Parts of this book were written in regional Queensland at a tiny historic cottage on a mountain lake. This beautiful place brought me so much joy, peace and inspiration, and it is with heartfelt gratitude that I will always associate this book with its magical essence. The lovely swans, wildflowers, stars and natural motifs that scatter these pages were drawn with poetic licence from my experience of this wonderful place, mixed with my hopes, dreams and visions for creating heaven on earth.

Last but not least, heartfelt thanks to you, dearest reader.
It brings me such delight to know this book has found its way into your hands.

Love, Meredith x

Published in 2021 by Hardie Grant Books,
an imprint of Hardie Grant Publishing

Hardie Grant Books (Melbourne)
Wurundjeri Country
Building 1, 658 Church Street
Richmond, Victoria 3121

Hardie Grant Books (London)
5th & 6th Floors
52-54 Southwark Street
London SE1 1UN

hardiegrantbooks.com

Relax
ISBN 978 1 74379 742 6

10 9 8 7 6 5 4 3 2 1

A catalogue record for this
book is available from the
National Library of Australia

Publisher: Pam Brewster
Project Editor: Joanna Wong
Editor: Allison Hiew
Designer: Mietta Yans
Production Manager: Todd Rechner

Colour reproduction by Splitting Image Colour Studio
Printed in China by Leo Paper Products LTD.

MIX
Paper from
responsible sources
FSC® C020056

The paper this book is printed on is from FSC®-certified
forests and other sources. FSC® promotes environmentally
responsible, socially beneficial and economically viable
management of the world's forests.